# Education After 16

Researched and written by Reference Services, Central Office of Information.

ISBN 0 11 701868 6

HMSO publications are available from:

**HMSO Publications Centre**
(Mail, fax and telephone orders only)
PO Box 276, London SW8 5DT
Telephone orders 0171-873 9090
General enquiries 0171-873 0011
(queuing system in operation for both numbers)
Fax orders 0171-873 8200

**HMSO Bookshops**
49 High Holborn, London WC1V 6HB
(counter service only)
0171-873 0011   Fax 0171-831 1326
68–69 Bull Street, Birmingham B4 6AD
0121-236 9696 Fax 0121-236 9699
33 Wine Street, Bristol BS1 2BQ
0117 9264306   Fax 0117 9294515
9-21 Princess Street, Manchester M60 8AS
0161-834 7201   Fax 0161-833 0634
16 Arthur Street, Belfast BT1 4GD
01232 238451   Fax 01232 235401
71 Lothian Road, Edinburgh EH3 9AZ
0131-228 4181   Fax 0131-229 2734

**HMSO's Accredited Agents**
(see Yellow Pages)

and through good booksellers

# Contents

# Acknowledgments

The Central Office of Information would like to thank the following organisations for their co-operation in compiling this book: the Business and Technology Education Council, City and Guilds of London Institute, Committee of Vice Chancellors and Principals of the United Kingdom Universities, Department for Education, Department of Education for Northern Ireland, Further Education Funding Council for England, National Council for Vocational Qualifications, RSA Examinations Board, Scottish Office Education Department, Scottish Vocational Education Council, Universities and Colleges Admissions Service, the Welsh Office and the Workers' Education Association.

## Cover Photograph Credit

Department for Education.

# Introduction

Education is compulsory up to the age of 16. After this students are educated in school sixth forms, sixth form colleges, further education colleges, universities and other higher education institutions. The former polytechnics have now become universities with the right to award their own degrees. Steps are being taken to give vocational qualifications the same status as academic ones. Further education colleges and sixth form colleges in England and Wales have become autonomous institutions outside local education authority control.

## Table 1: Full- and Part-time Higher Education Students in Great Britain

|  | 1982–83 | 1992–93 | % Increase |
|---|---|---|---|
| **Full-time** |  |  |  |
| Postgraduate | 57,100 | 102,400 | 79 |
| First degree | 407,900 | 687,000 | 68 |
| Other undergraduate | 88,000 | 144,800 | 65 |
| **Part-time** |  |  |  |
| Postgraduate | 42,900 | 110,700 | 158 |
| First degree | 88,700 | 148,200 | 67 |
| Other undergraduate | 165,000 | 215,800 | 31 |
| Total | 849,700 | 1,408,000 | 66 |

Higher education consists of degree and other courses of a standard higher than the General Certificate of Education (GCE) Advanced (A) level or its equivalent (see p. 12).

The number of full- and part-time students enrolled in higher education courses in 1992–93 was over 1.4 million in Great Britain,[1] a 60 per cent increase since 1982–83. There were 34,713 higher education students in Northern Ireland in 1992–93. Women make up 47 per cent of higher education students.

Further education comprises courses up to and including GCE A level or GNVQ Advanced level. The table below shows the number of students in 1992–93.

### Students Enrolled on Further and Adult Education Courses in 1992–93 (Great Britain)

| | |
|---|---|
| England | 3,372,000 |
| Scotland | 310,449 |
| Wales | 202,868 |
| Total | 3,885,317 |

*Note*: In Northern Ireland 84,808 people were enrolled on vocational further education courses and 44,917 on non-vocational courses.

The further and higher education systems in England, Wales and Northern Ireland are virtually identical, although there are some differences in funding the system in Northern Ireland. Those in Scotland, although sharing some similarities, have clear differences in organisation, especially in courses, qualifications and the funding of further education.

---

[1] 'Britain' is used informally in this book to mean the United Kingdom of Great Britain and Northern Ireland. 'Great Britain' comprises England, Wales and Scotland.

# Further Education

## History

In the early 19th century the mechanics institute movement, which was the predecessor of the vocational education movement, began to spread, its aim being to help train industrial workers. It had its origins in Scotland and began work in London in 1823; at the movement's zenith there were over 700 mechanics institutes, mainly located in manufacturing regions.

The further education system developed in the latter years of the 19th century as rapid advances in science and technology led to a need for more skilled and qualified workers. Alongside traditional academic institutions like the older universities in England, Scotland and Wales, provision was made for vocational training in trades and professions.

Stimulated by the 1851 Great Exhibition in London, technical education began developing, an important step being the foundation of the City and Guilds of London Institute in 1878 to provide education for people in manufacturing and other industries. The Institute financed evening classes for workers and organised examinations on technical subjects throughout Britain. In 1883 the Finsbury Technical College was opened under City and Guilds auspices in order to educate people preparing for jobs in industry. This college was a forerunner of many more in the industrial towns, some developing from mechanics institutes.

Legislation passed in 1889 gave local government authorities the optional power to levy a penny rate to finance technical or manual instruction. The new county and county borough councils provided technical education in day and evening classes.

The twentieth century saw a massive expansion in further education. Evening institutes were founded in 1926 to provide facilities for adults to study in the evenings, with classes being held in day schools and other educational buildings. In addition, colleges of further education spread throughout Britain, offering full-time and part-time courses for young people, adults and evening students, a pattern that has persisted to the present day.

The 1944 Education Act made it obligatory for local education authorities to provide further/technical education. In the 1980s and early 1990s polytechnics and further education colleges in Great Britain became autonomous institutions and the polytechnics achieved university status.

## Nature of Further Education

Although compulsory school education ends at the age of 16, many young people choose to remain at school, in most cases to study for qualifications leading to entry to universities and other higher education institutions.

Other 16-year-olds choose to leave school and pursue their studies in further education colleges, which provide General Certificate of Education (GCE) A and AS (Advanced Supplementary) level courses, along with a wide range of vocational courses; some of these vocational courses can also be taken in schools and in sixth form colleges. Vocational courses lead to nationally recognised qualifications (see p. 13). There are over 500 further education colleges in England and Wales and 43 in Scotland. Northern Ireland has 24 colleges, 12 of which are being merged into 5 new institutions, leaving a total of 17 colleges. Further education institutions range from specialist colleges with fewer than 250 students to multi-disciplinary colleges with several thousands.

Most further education is work-related and vocational, although the majority of colleges also provide non-vocational courses, including General Certificate of Secondary Education (GCSE) and GCE A level courses. A wide range of courses are available at all levels and offer students the opportunity to progress from one qualification to the next and to study a mix of academic and vocational courses. There are full-time and part-time day and evening study and intensive short courses. Some courses use audio-visual techniques and correspondence as teaching methods. The system is flexible and enables the student to acquire the qualification appropriate to his or her needs. Typical courses cover subjects like information technology, computing, business studies, electronics, foreign languages, art and design, engineering, construction and office administration. Facilities are available to students with disabilities or learning difficulties. The system has strong ties with industry and commerce, with employers being involved in designing courses.

## Colleges

Further education colleges and sixth form colleges are autonomous, having been released from local education authority control in April 1993. Each college is conducted by a corporation with its own legal identity. Colleges employ their own staff, manage their assets and resources, contract to provide services to employers and other clients and take part in joint enterprises with industry or local authorities. There are no sixth form colleges in Northern Ireland.

The college governing body is responsible for carrying out these functions. It must also ensure that relevant and up-to-date courses are run in the interests of students, local business and the local community. They must be run in accordance with sound business principles and give value for money, and are empowered to earn income through provision of courses, consultancy, curriculum packages and open learning facilities.

At least half of governing body members must have experience of industry, commerce or the professions. The other members may be drawn from staff, students and the local community.

## Government Responsibilities

The Department for Education in England, the Welsh Office Education Department, the Scottish Office Education Department and the Department of Education for Northern Ireland are responsible for securing the provision of adequate further education. Their functions include:

—formulating general further education policy; and

—providing resources to the further education funding councils.

### Funding Councils in England and Wales

Government funds for colleges in England and Wales are distributed by two further education funding councils. The remainder of college income comes mainly from charges made for services to students and employers.

The English Further Education Funding Council consists of members with a background in education as well as those from industry, commerce and the professions. The Government is also entitled to be represented at Council meetings. The Council has a number of regional committees to advise on local issues. The committees work closely with the locally based Training and Enterprise Councils, which are responsible for promoting more effective training by employers and individuals.

The English Funding Council is responsible for allocating over £2,000 million each year to the colleges. It has a statutory duty to secure provision of sufficient further education facilities throughout the country and must have regard to the needs of people with learning difficulties. This means that full-time courses must be available for all 16- to 18-year-olds who want them. In addition, the Council has to ensure that adequate part-time education is provided for people aged 16 and over, as well as full-time education for those aged 19 or over, leading to academic and vocational qualifications and other provision. The Council inspects colleges and its quality assessment committee advises it on the quality of education provided by them. A majority of committee members have further education experience.

The Council is accountable to the Secretary of State for the funds made available to it by the Government.

Recurrent funds consist of two elements:

—a block grant for distribution to colleges by the Council; and

—separate funds directly related to student numbers, intended to be a financial incentive to colleges to recruit more students.

Colleges also receive capital funds for buildings and equipment.

Fees are not charged to 16- to 18-year-olds receiving full-time education in the colleges.

The Further Education Funding Council for Wales operates on a similar basis to the English Funding Council.

The Further Education Unit, financed by the English and Welsh Further Education Councils, reviews and supports curriculum development and promotes quality of learning. Much of the Unit's work consists of research and development projects, on which reports are published. Impartial and practical advice, based on the research, is given to national education organisations and policymakers. The Unit is managed by an independent Board of

Management whose members are appointed by the Secretary of State. The Further Education Development Association will supersede the Further Education Unit and the Further Education Staff College in 1995. The Association will support and develop the management of learning in order to secure improvements in the quality of further education.

### Scotland and Northern Ireland

In Scotland public funds are provided to colleges by the Scottish Office Education Department.

The Scottish Further Education Unit was set up to improve the vocational education and training system. It helps implement national education and training initiatives and provides a forum for discussion and action. Guidance is provided on college curricula. It is partly financed by the Scottish Office Education Department but also generates income through other activities.

In Northern Ireland colleges are funded entirely by the Government through five local education and library boards responsible for providing adequate further education provision in their areas. Since 1991, colleges have taken on more responsibility for managing their own budgets and increased their efforts to generate additional income. These responsibilities have recently been extended to enable colleges to set up companies. In addition, further education colleges are recognised training organisations for the purposes of the Youth Training Programme run by the Training and Employment Agency.

## Students

Students aged between 16 and 18 who wish to study full-time are entitled to free education, including tuition, or training in a school or college. If students wish to study part-time or are 19 or over, they may have to pay fees. Colleges have to provide information about the charges for each course. Students studying for a National Vocational Qualification (NVQ) at levels 1–4 or a General National Vocational Qualification (GNVQ—see p. 13) are entitled to tax relief if they are paying their own course fees. This means that students pay 75 per cent of the college course fees; the remaining 25 per cent is claimed by the college from the Inland Revenue.

Other financial support for further education students includes discretionary awards from local education authorities, limited access funds provided by colleges (see p. 7) and financial assistance by employers (see p. 59).

Under the Government's various charters for further and higher education, prospective students can expect to have access to free and accurate information from each college about:

—entry requirements;

—courses and qualifications;

—the type of teaching and assessment on each course; and

—the scope for building up credits towards a qualification.

Colleges are also expected to supply information about their approach to students with learning difficulties and disabilities, including provision of extra staff and equipment and arrangements for access to buildings.

Students are entitled to equal treatment regardless of gender or ethnic background. Marital status, too, must not affect the way students are treated. They have the right to expect colleges to explain what they are doing to foster equal opportunities by, for example, providing childcare facilities.

People applying for places in colleges are provided with information about how well colleges are doing. This includes:

—comparative summaries of examination and other results, published by the government education departments, for all colleges and school sixth forms; and

—annual details from each college about its results and what its students go on to do when they leave.

The first comparative performance tables on GCE A and AS examination results and their vocational equivalents in England and Wales were published in November 1993 in 24 booklets, each covering several local education authority areas. Schools have been asked to ensure that they give a copy of the tables to all their pupils in the final year of compulsory education.

Information is available about the English and Welsh Funding Councils' independent inspection reports on standards achieved in particular subjects and colleges, together with the college's response to the report. Students' views are taken into account during the inspections. Reports are published every four years on the quality of the education provided by each college. Lists of recent reports are available from schools, colleges, public libraries and careers offices. On request, the college gives students a summary of any relevant funding council report and its response.

In Scotland Her Majesty's Inspectorate is responsible for monitoring the performance of further education colleges; regular inspections take place and reports are published on the results. Students' views are sought during the inspections and published reports are available to students from the college.

Students have the right to expect high quality teaching, subject to this independent inspection, and to make their views known about it. Colleges must ensure that:

—all courses meet the assessment requirements for the qualification in question;

—qualifications have value outside the college itself;

—work placements for students are well-prepared and suitable for the course;

—students and their employers receive regular progress reports, including relevant coursework assessment; and

—achievements are assessed and recorded at the end of the study period.

Colleges are expected to conduct an annual survey of the views of their student and employer customers and make a summary of the findings available.

## Complaints Systems

If a student is dissatisfied with the services provided by a further education college, he or she can complain to the college. If the student is unhappy with the college response, he or she can complain to the appropriate Further Education Funding Council or, as a last resort, to the Secretary of State. In Scotland students can complain to the Secretary of State.

If the student is unhappy about the quality of a particular qualification, he or she can complain to the awarding or accrediting body. Complaints about results are dealt with by the awarding body through the college.

## Student Bodies

Most colleges have a student body responsible for providing services such as welfare, catering, sport and representation within the college (see also p. 56).

# Courses and Qualifications

## England, Wales and Northern Ireland

There are three types of qualification available for the 16 to 18 age group:

—GCE A level and AS level examinations taken after two years' full-time study:

—GNVQs, providing vocational qualifications for young people in full-time education; and

—NVQs, which are mainly for those who have left full-time education.

Efforts are being made to ensure that academic and vocational qualifications have equal status.

### GCE A and AS Levels

The GCE A level examination is taken by students usually at 18 or 19 years of age and provides entry to higher education. There are five pass grades—A to E. The AS level enables students to pursue a wider range of subject areas, for example by combining science or arts subjects. Two AS levels are equivalent to one A level and are accepted as such for university entrance. Courses consist of a combination of internally assessed coursework and externally assessed examinations. Some courses are made up of units of study called modules.

A and AS examinations are set by the GCE examining boards. The School Curriculum and Assessment Authority is responsible for approving the boards' examination syllabuses and maintaining standards. Under the Authority's principles, syllabuses must:

—ensure that students experience disciplined study of a subject in proper breadth, balance and depth;

—specify learning and assessment requirements;

—ensure that any course made up of units is coherent and to the same standard as other A and AS level courses; and

—provide a proper basis for further study at degree level or equivalent.

The Authority's guidelines say that the titles of A and AS level syllabuses and qualifications should give a clear and accurate indication of the subject matter studied. AS syllabuses should set out their relationship with A levels of the same title.

On the question of assessment, the Authority wants this to be:

—valid and reliable, with consistently applied procedures covering all aspects of the examination process; and

—predominantly by means of externally assessed examinations.

Coursework, the Authority's principles state, should be externally assessed and, in most subjects, limited to a maximum of 20 per cent of the total available marks. The Authority and the examining boards have agreed that coursework should form a higher percentage of work in practical subjects, for example, 60 per cent in art and design, 40 per cent in computing and 50 per cent in music.

The Northern Ireland Council for the Curriculum, Examinations and Assessment conducts examinations, administers and moderates formal assessments and advises the Department of Education on curriculum matters.

*General National Vocational Qualification*
The General National Vocational Qualification is a new qualification taken mainly by students in schools and colleges. It was originally developed for the 16 to 19 age group, although it is also available for adults. There are also plans for GNVQs to be available in schools for 14- to 16-year-olds. The main purpose of the new qualification is to provide a genuine vocational alternative to traditional academic qualifications for the increasing number of students staying on in full-time education beyond the age of 16. The Government wants to see 25 per cent of 16-year-olds starting GNVQs by 1996. In the longer term the aim is that half of all 16- and 17-year-olds should take GNVQs.

GNVQs provide a broad-based education designed to develop a range of fundamental skills and the application of knowledge and understanding to an occupational sector. As well as acquiring the basic skills and knowledge underpinning a vocational area, students are expected to demonstrate core skills which prepare them for work or further study. All GNVQs consist of units, each of which is assessed through assignment work and, in the case of mandatory units, an externally set test. Completed GNVQs are graded at pass, merit and distinction.

GNVQs, which must first be approved by the National Council for Vocational Qualifications, are available at three levels—Foundation, Intermediate and Advanced—and are offered by the Business and Technology Education Council, City and Guilds of London Institute and the RSA Examinations Board (see p. 22).

Following a trial year in 1992–93, many schools and colleges began offering Advanced and Intermediate GNVQs in:

—art and design;

—business;

—health and social care;

—leisure and tourism; and

—manufacturing.

From September 1994, further GNVQs at Intermediate and Advanced levels were made widely available in built environment, hospitality and catering, and science. GNVQs in information technology, engineering, media and communication, distribution, and management will be piloted with a view to them becoming generally available from September 1995. The land-based industries GNVQ will be piloted from September 1995 for introduction in 1996.

It is intended that the Advanced GNVQ and A levels will soon have equal status in the eyes of employers and higher education institutions. Many students will be able to take a mix of GCE A levels and Advanced GNVQs.

The Advanced GNVQ, which will usually take two years to complete, consists of eight mandatory units, plus four optional units from a list of eight choices. Mandatory units cover the fundamental skills, knowledge, understanding and principles common to a wide range of related occupations. In addition there are core skill units covering communication, numeracy and information technology (see below) which are integrated within the mandatory units. Students may also gain additional units in such subjects as foreign languages and mathematics. Mandatory and core skill units are devised centrally and have the same content, irrespective of the body awarding the qualification. Optional and additional units are developed separately by the awarding bodies.

The Intermediate GNVQ, which is normally a one-year programme, consists of six vocational units, including four mandatory units and two optional units from a list of four choices. The three core skill units cover the same subjects as those for the Advanced level. The Intermediate GNVQ is generally regarded as being equivalent to four GCSE passes at grades A, B and C. The linked design of the two levels enables schools and colleges to offer students clear routes of progression and widens student choice.

The Foundation GNVQ is broadly equivalent to GCSEs at grades D to G and consists of three mandatory plus three optional vocational units and the three core skill units. Unlike the Advanced and Intermediate levels, students can choose optional units from different vocational areas.

The core skill unit in communication covers:

—participation in discussions;

—preparing written materials;

—using images to illustrate points made in writing and discussion; and

—reading and responding to written materials and images.

The key themes in the application of the core skill unit in numeracy include:

—gathering and processing data;

—representing and tackling problems; and

—interpreting and presenting data.

The information technology core skill unit covers:

—storing and inputting information;

—editing and organising information;

—presenting information;

—evaluating procedures and features of applications; and

—dealing with errors and faults.

*National Vocational Qualifications*

A new system of NVQs is being introduced in order to raise the standard of people's competence at work.

NVQs are based on standards developed by industry and commerce and have the full support of employers and trade unions as well as the bodies which award vocational qualifications (see p. 19). The National Council for Vocational Qualifications is responsible for implementing the new system and approving awarding bodies.

All NVQs are slotted into the NVQ Framework, which has five levels of achievement:

Level 1—Foundation

Level 2—Basic craft

Level 3—Technician, advanced craft, supervisor

Level 4—Higher technician, junior management

Level 5—Professional, middle management.

Each NVQ consists of a number of separate units setting out standards for the broad skills required for a job. Unlike traditional qualifications, NVQs test the ability to do a job and are assessed in workplace conditions; in addition they are often tested by practical, oral or written examinations. Units can be followed one at a time or in any combination until the qualification is achieved. Although NVQs can also be taken in colleges and occasionally at school, work-based experience is always required.

NVQ standards are packaged into qualifications by awarding bodies. The National Council for Vocational Qualifications decides whether qualifications follow NVQ criteria. If they do, the Council approves the award, which then becomes an NVQ.

If a qualification is to be accredited as an NVQ by the Council, it must be:

—based on national standards;

—awarded on the basis of valid and reliable assessments;

—free from barriers restricting access and progression; and

—free from overt or covert discriminatory practices regarding gender, age, race or creed.

The National Council is responsible for ensuring that awarding bodies have adequate arrangements for assuring quality. Annual reports are made by the awarding body to the National Council on the efficiency of this monitoring. In future the National

Council has plans to use external consultants to look in detail at various aspects of assessment.

The National Database of Vocational Qualifications is the most authoritative and up-to-date information source for qualifications. It provides information on NVQs and other available qualifications, the units required and the composition of each unit. It is used by schools, further education colleges and universities.

The Government has drawn up a series of National Targets for Education and Training, based on NVQs and designed to raise standards. The key foundation learning targets are as follows:

—by 1997, 80 per cent of young people to reach NVQ Level 2 or equivalent:

—training and education to NVQ Level 3 or equivalent to be available to all young people who can benefit;

—by 2000, 50 per cent of young people to reach NVQ Level 3 or equivalent; and

—education and training to develop self-reliance, flexibility and breadth of study.

There are also a number of targets for lifetime learning. According to these:

—by 1996, all employees should take part in training or development activities;

—by 1996, 50 per cent of the employed workforce should aim for NVQs or units towards them; and

—by 2000, 50 per cent of the employed workforce should be qualified to at least NVQ Level 3 or equivalent.

The National Advisory Council on Education and Training Targets, comprising leading representatives from employers, education and trade unions, is responsible for monitoring progress towards the Targets and advising the Government on performance and policies which influence this progress. The Council is also concerned with raising skill levels and increasing employer commitment to the Targets. It reports annually on progress made towards the Targets.

The Advisory Scottish Council for Education and Training Targets has been set up in Scotland to monitor and report on progress.

In 1995 a new modern apprenticeship scheme is being introduced to increase the number of young people trained to technician, supervisory and equivalent levels. When the scheme is fully in operation, about 150,000 young people in England are expected to be in training.

**Awarding Bodies**

About 90 per cent of vocational qualifications are awarded by three examining bodies in England, Wales and Northern Ireland. The remainder are awarded by professional bodies and some other organisations.

*Business and Technology Education Council (BTEC)*
The BTEC was originally established by the Government to promote and develop high-quality work-related educational programmes. Main subject areas include agriculture, business and finance, caring, computing, construction, design, distribution, engineering, hotel and catering, leisure, travel and tourism, science and management.

BTEC GNVQs at Advanced and Intermediate levels are being introduced over a three-year period. As appropriate GNVQs and NVQs become available, corresponding BTEC First, National and Higher National qualifications will be phased out. BTEC Firsts and Nationals will, however, continue to be offered for part-time students.

BTEC First Programmes are normally taken by school leavers or sixth formers who have chosen the general area of work they wish to enter. The First Diploma Programme is a one-year course of full-time study while the First Certificate Programme is a one-year part-time course. There are no formal entry requirements. These first qualifications can lead on to employment, to BTEC National Programmes or BTEC GNVQ level 3.

BTEC National Programmes are for people intending to become junior managers or administrators and technicians. The BTEC National Diploma takes two years' full-time or three years' part-time study. The BTEC National Certificate takes two years of part-time study. These BTEC National qualifications can lead on to employment or higher education degree courses.

Some students decide to go on to BTEC Higher National Programmes qualifying them to work at managerial, supervisory and higher technician levels. The Higher National Diploma takes two years full-time or three years part-time, while the Higher National Certificate takes two years of part-time study. Holders of BTEC Higher National qualifications can often be admitted to the second or third year of a degree course in a related subject.

BTEC courses are based on units or modules, all of which must be passed by the student. They are available in over 1,000 schools, colleges and universities in England, Wales and Northern Ireland.

*City and Guilds of London Institute*
Founded in 1878 by the Corporation of the City of London and some of the livery companies (see p. 3), the City and Guilds of

London Institute (C & G) is an independent organisation operating under Royal Charter. In 1990 it acquired the Pitman Examinations Institute. C & G awards nationally recognised certificates in over 400 subjects, many of which are NVQs. It also awards a full range of GNVQs at Foundation, Intermediate and Advanced levels.

The awards structure spans seven levels, from foundation to the highest level of professional competence. Awards are available for secondary school pupils, young people in further education, employees wanting to improve skills, people returning to work who need retraining and adult learners.

C & G schemes are assessed in a number of ways. For NVQs and other vocational qualifications, the most commonly used method is workplace observation by supervisors and managers with experience of the work under observation. Other schemes are assessed by:

—written papers;

—multiple-choice questions;

—assignments;

—oral questioning;

—projects; or

—any combination of these.

Most schemes consist of a number of compulsory core units, plus a wider range of units giving candidates the right to choose subjects most relevant to their area of study or specialisation. They work at their own pace towards the full award.

C & G senior awards recognise significant achievements made by individuals in their area of work. They offer an employment-based, rather than academic, route to professional qualifications.

Before any establishment can offer courses leading to C & G qualifications, it must be able to demonstrate that it has qualified and experienced staff. C & G employs subject experts who visit schools, colleges, training centres, companies and adult education institutes in order to make sure that quality of provision is maintained.

*RSA Examinations Board*
The RSA Examinations Board offers NVQs in:

—business administration;

—retail and wholesale distribution;

—financial services, including accountancy and insurance;

—information technology;

—journalism;

—foreign languages;

—management; and

—training and development.

Once the GNVQ system is fully implemented, the RSA will offer all these subjects as GNVQs (see p. 13).

Candidates for RSA qualifications are examined and assessed by teachers and trainers working part-time. Methods of assessment include work-based measures, projects, assignments, oral tests and case studies; these are often used as part of a continuous assessment programme subject to rigorous verification by RSA staff.

*Agriculture*
Another awarding body is the National Examinations Board for Agriculture, Horticulture and Allied Industries, which is the largest testing and awarding organisation for these areas. It offers assessments and awards at all levels from basic skills tests to management level qualifications. Awards include many NVQs and

National and Advanced National Certificates in agriculture, horticulture and floristry. Board qualifications are available in over 200
centres and are supported by City and Guilds assessment, administration and quality control systems.

## Scotland

Most vocational qualifications in Scotland are accredited and
awarded by the Scottish Vocational Education Council
(SCOTVEC), which works in partnership with colleges, business
and government in order to ensure that its courses are relevant and
flexible enough to respond to change. It is responsible for developing and maintaining a coherent system of skill-based vocational
qualifications. The validation system ensures that all its units and
group awards (see below) contain clear statements of what successful candidates should be able to do. Colleges, schools and other
training centres have to be approved by SCOTVEC if they wish to
offer its qualifications. All SCOTVEC-approved centres are visited by specialists drawn from education, training, industry and
commerce; they ensure that national standards are applied consistently and offer advice and guidance to staff.

The main SCOTVEC qualifications are the National
Certificate; the Higher National Certificate and the Higher
National Diploma; Scottish Vocational Qualifications (SVQs); and
General Scottish Vocational Qualifications (GSVQs). SCOTVEC
also offers Professional Development Awards which span a wide
variety of occupational areas. Other awards are tailored to the needs
of specific employers.

SCOTVEC qualifications are based on a flexible system of
nationally recognised units of study called modules, each of which
involves about 40 hours of study of a particular topic. Assessment

is continuous, the student having to demonstrate ability as he or she progresses. Modules can be taken individually or in groups. Each unit achieved is listed on a SCOTVEC Record of Education and Training. Modules have been developed after extensive consultations with people in industry to ensure that they respond to the requirements of employers.

*National Certificate*
The National Certificate has some 3,000 modules covering the vast majority of occupations, including engineering and science, computing, secretarial and office skills, art and photography, music and languages. Clusters of modules are available to help students, especially school pupils, to make their choice from the modules available. Each cluster is a group of three module credits. Modules in each cluster are specially chosen to form a coherent package designed to assist students to go on to further study or to employment. The clusters have been developed by SCOTVEC and the Scottish Consultative Council on the Curriculum.

National Certificate modules can also be built up to form GSVQs, which form a broad introduction to vocational subjects like information technology, business administration, science and design. GSVQs are available at three levels: National Certificate level I, National Certificate level II and National Certificate level III. All GSVQs incorporate the core skills of communication, information technology, personal and interpersonal skills, numeracy and problem-solving.

GSVQs are designed to fit into the overall framework of SCOTVEC qualifications and offer progression to Higher National Certificates, Higher National Diplomas and Scottish Vocational Qualifications (SVQ—see p. 27). They are broadly compatible with the GNVQs available in England, Wales and Northern Ireland.

Another kind of National Certificate group award, Skillstart, helps students take their first step up the ladder of SCOTVEC qualifications. Skillstart 1 is designed for slower learners, offering them the opportunity to gain a qualification recognising their abilities. Skillstart 2 is for those without any formal qualifications and is designed to help them gain one which can improve their job prospects or chances of entering further training or education.

*Higher National Units*

The advanced courses offered by colleges are made up of a group of Higher National Units, which are free-standing units of study designed to take about 40 hours. The student must be able to demonstrate ability in a specified list of skills. Higher National Units are more advanced than National Certificate modules and cover subjects like business administration, information and office management, engineering and electrical engineering. The courses are widely recognised for entry to employment at higher technician or junior management level. They are also accepted for admission to many degree courses and often make it possible for a student to go straight into the second or third year of a degree course.

*Professional Development Awards*

SCOTVEC also offers a range of Professional Development Awards. They can be used to build on existing qualifications and are offered in areas like computing, engineering practice and business counselling.

The Advanced Diploma is for those who have a Higher National Diploma in the same discipline. It consists of more than

12 Higher National Unit credits and can provide direct access to a master's degree or equivalent.

The Diploma is a qualification at Higher National Certificate level for those with a degree or a diploma in a different discipline. It normally consists of ten or more Higher National unit credits.

The Advanced Certificate is designed to develop competence demonstrated by a candidate in National Certificate programmes. It normally consists of between six and 12 Higher National Unit credits.

The Certificate can be made up of National Certificate modules, Higher National units or workplace assessed units. The number of credits for each Certificate varies according to the nature of the award.

*Higher Still*

The age group 16–18 has a choice of academic and vocational courses. The academic ones are the responsibility of the Scottish Examinations Board (SEB); called Highers, they are the equivalent of the GCE A level in England, Wales and Northern Ireland. SCOTVEC is responsible for the vocational courses.

A new unified framework of courses and awards for education in schools and colleges for the 16–18 age group will take effect in the late 1990s. This will combine SEB and SCOTVEC courses, including Highers and GSVQs in a unified curriculum and assessment system so that students can study vocational and academic courses of equal standing. The recommended study time for each Higher will be extended from 120 to 160 hours and Higher courses will consist of modules. Advanced Higher courses will be developed, incorporating the current Certificate of Sixth Year Studies, and will build on Highers in order to provide a two-year 320-hour course.

Students will be able to take whatever mix of academic and vocational courses they wish and gain qualifications in the form of National Certificates or Highers and Advanced Highers, all of which will lead to acceptable entrance requirements for higher education.

*Scottish Vocational Qualifications*
Introduced in 1989, SVQs meet standards set by industry and are accepted as a guarantee of an applicant's ability to do a particular job. Over 400 are available in areas including agriculture, banking, business administration, computing, management, retailing and social and health care. SVQs are recognised throughout Britain since they are analogous with the NVQs available in England, Wales and Scotland. They can be built up from SCOTVEC National Certificate modules, Higher National units and workplace assessed units, or a combination of these. SVQs have five levels similar to those of the NVQ system.

Although SVQs are commonly acquired through learning and training, they can also be obtained on the basis of evidence of prior learning and achievement. All SVQs are assessed in the workplace or under workplace conditions. They are frequently offered through a partnership between employers and further education colleges. Standards are developed nationally by some 180 recognised industry bodies. SCOTVEC requires that those responsible for assessment should be properly trained to do the job and have knowledge of the occupational area concerned. Certificates are issued to assessors who meet the necessary requirements, thereby ensuring quality in the delivery of SVQs. Any centre—be it a company, a training unit or a college—can seek approval from SCOTVEC to issue these certificates.

The Government is committed to Scottish Education and Training Targets, under which 85 per cent of young people should reach SVQ2 or its academic equivalent by 2000, with 70 per cent of young people reaching SVQ3 or its academic equivalent within the same timetable.

*SCOTVEC Validation System*
SCOTVEC's validation system ensures that all its units and group awards contain clear statements setting out requirements for successful candidates. It also approves colleges, schools and other training centres wishing to offer its qualifications. They must meet SCOTVEC requirements on staffing and other resources. SCOTVEC-approved establishments are visited by verifiers drawn from education and training, industry and commerce. They ensure that national standards are applied and offer advice and guidance to staff.

*Qualifications Database*
A database maintained by the Scottish Further Education Unit provides the most up-to-date information on vocational qualifications as well as general guidance information. It is widely used by Local Enterprise Companies (LECs—see below), further education colleges, career services and schools.

*Employment-based Training*
LECs operate programmes of work-based training and retraining, many of which lead to recognised vocational qualifications. Long and short programmes are offered for adults in jobs, self-employed people and those without a job. Programme priorities are decided locally. They cover:

A computer laboratory being used by European Studies students at the University College, Stockton, founded as the result of collaboration between Durham and Teesside Universities.

A technician at work in the tropical house of Durham University's Botanic Gardens, which are used in environmental and biological projects.

Training for an NVQ in Playwork, organised by City and Guilds. Playworkers help children with out-of-school play activities, and can work in a variety of settings, including adventure playgrounds, play centres and city farms.

The annual fashion show at Middlesex University, which offers an Honours degree in the subject.

City and Guilds

The City and Guilds course in Motor Vehicle Craft Studies involves the repair, testing and maintenance of all types of motor vehicles, including cars and public service vehicles.

A level art students at St Joseph's Roman Catholic High School, Newport, Gwent.

Format

NVQs in Administration provide candidates with the range of skills they need to work in a wide variety of jobs across all employment sectors.

British universities offer a wide variety of degrees with music as either the major discipline or forming part of a multi-disciplinary degree.

—business management;

—business growth;

—enterprise training for self-employment;

—training for supervisors and workplace trainers;

—specialised skills training; and

—training to help unemployed people get back to work.

LECs are represented on the boards of management of all further education colleges and are important customers of the colleges. They are responsible for providing Youth Training for young people under 18 who are not in full-time education or employment. Training courses lead to SVQs (or their equivalents) at level 2 or above. Training for SVQs can be supplemented by training designed to develop general skills such as communication, numeracy, problem-solving and information technology. A training credit scheme will be phased in by 1996; this is an entitlement to vocational education and training for young people leaving full-time education at 16 or 17. The credit enables the young person to purchase training or education from colleges in the form of an SVQ to level 2 or above.

## Further Education for Adults

Adult continuing education is provided in further education colleges, adult colleges and centres and by voluntary bodies. Responsibility for adult education provision in England and Wales is divided between the further education funding councils and LEAs. The former are responsible for courses leading to academic and vocational qualifications, basic skills courses, English as a second language courses and courses on communications skills for students with learning difficulties. LEAs are responsible for securing other types of education for adults such as leisure time courses and cultural and craft pursuits.

In addition to mature students taking degree courses, universities have continuing education departments which provide non-degree courses for adults in their spare time.

**Adult Literacy and Basic Skills Unit**

The Adult Literacy and Basic Skills Unit (ALBSU) was established in England and Wales by the Government in 1980 to act as the main focus for adult literacy, numeracy and related skills. The Unit:

—provides consultancy and advisory services;

—funds a substantial number of development projects, including research;

—produces and publishes material for teachers and students; and

—organises and sponsors staff training.

The Basic Skills at Work Programme, announced in 1991, encourages local education authorities, Training and Enterprise Councils and local employers to work together to improve basic skills by funding 40 development initiatives. The programme is aimed at unemployed people and those in work who cannot progress without improved basic skills. It is overseen by ALBSU and is supported by the Department for Education, the Employment Department and the Welsh Office.

The Department's grant to ALBSU in 1994–95 was £4,649,000, of which £3,193,000 was the core grant. An additional £260,000 was made available to the Basic Skills at Work Programme, which is aimed at unemployed people and those in work who cannot progress without improved skills. Some

£1.2 million was allocated to the family literacy scheme, which seeks to break the intergenerational cycle of reading failure by raising children's and parents' attainments.

## National Organisation of Adult Learning

The National Organisation of Adult Learning—formerly the National Institute of Adult Continuing Education and still known as NIACE—is the national body representing adult learners in England and Wales. It convenes conferences, seminars and meetings, collects and disseminates information, conducts enquiries and research, undertakes special projects and works with other organisations.

## Open and Distance Learning

The term 'open and distance learning' broadly means learning undertaken without the regular direct supervision of a tutor, through use of various media such as television. More and more further education colleges are incorporating many distance learning materials and methods in their mainstream courses, thereby allowing increasing numbers of students to learn in ways which suit them best.

Open learning opportunities in further education were extended in 1987 by the formation of the Open College, an independent company set up with Government support which brings together broadcasters, educationalists and sponsors. It provides vocational education and training courses below degree level. The Open College of the Arts, also launched in 1987, offers foundation courses in the arts to those wishing to study at home.

## Scottish Community Education Council

The Scottish Community Education Council advises the Government and promotes all community education matters, including adult literacy, basic education and the youth service in Scotland.

## Workers' Educational Association

The Workers' Educational Association (WEA), founded in 1903 as a partnership between universities, trade unions and the Co-operative movement, is the largest voluntary adult education organisation in Britain. About 145,000 students attend WEA courses each year, classes covering academic, recreational and vocational subjects. The WEA organises courses for the Trades Union Congress and individual trade unions. In addition to the income received from course fees, the WEA receives grants from public funds. Courses are organised by 14 district offices and 650 branches. The WEA is particularly concerned with people who are socially, economically and educationally disadvantaged, the aim being to increase their confidence and give them the necessary skills to proceed to colleges or universities.

# Higher Education

Higher education consists of courses of a standard higher than GCE A level or equivalent. It is available in universities and other higher education institutions.

The Secretary of State for Education is responsible for higher education policy in England. This function is the responsibility of the Secretaries of State for Scotland, Wales and Northern Ireland in their respective countries. They set out the overall policy for higher education in their respective areas and determine the level of public funding. The latter accounts for 65 per cent of university income, the rest consisting of fees from students and grants from research councils and private sources.

Higher education institutions are responsible for their own admissions policies, determining the length and content of courses, and, in many cases, awarding their own degrees. They fall into two categories:

—universities offering mainly first degree courses for undergraduates and degrees for postgraduates; and

—colleges and institutes of higher education, some of which are multi-disciplinary while others specialise in a single area of study such as teacher training.

Higher education institutions are independent under the law and are free from government control. The Government has no power to intervene on matters such as admissions, the content of courses or teaching methods.

# University Development

The oldest universities in England and Wales, Oxford and Cambridge, were founded in the 12th and 13th centuries. In Oxford University, Balliol and Merton Colleges were founded between 1249 and 1264, followed by New College in 1370. By the middle of the 16th century others had opened, including All Souls (1437), Magdalen (1458) and Christchurch (1546). The residential college system also developed in Cambridge, starting with Peterhouse in 1284, followed by Clare (1326), King's (1441) and Trinity (1546). Today Oxford has 35 colleges and Cambridge 31.

In Scotland the oldest university is St Andrews, founded in 1411. Glasgow University dates from 1451, Aberdeen University from 1495 and Edinburgh University from 1583.

The industrial revolution of the 19th century led to increasing urbanisation of the population. Advances made in science and technology and improved literacy increased demand for university education. The University of London was given a Royal Charter in 1836 and it set out to provide an institution open to all, regardless of race, creed or political belief. Religious tests for university entrance elsewhere were gradually abandoned and finally abolished by 1871. In 1837 the University of Durham received its Charter.

The second half of the 19th and the first half of the 20th centuries saw an expansion of university education in the new centres of population. From the start they were secular institutions created to fill local needs and placed emphasis on the study of science and technology, although they now offer a full range of courses. They were originally founded as university colleges, granting external degrees of the University of London. Subsequently they received their Royal Charters as full degree-granting universities. Before 1914, universities were set up in Manchester, Liverpool, Bristol,

Leeds, Sheffield and Birmingham. In 1926 Reading's university college became a university.

Other university colleges achieved university status after the second world war—Nottingham in 1948, Southampton in 1952, Hull in 1954, Exeter in 1955 and Leicester in 1957. In 1963 the Newcastle division of Durham University was established as a separate university.

The federal University of Wales was founded in 1893. In 1908 the Queen's University of Belfast was given university status, having been founded in 1845.

In the 1960s some completely new universities were established, including Stirling, Sussex, East Anglia, Essex, Lancaster, Kent and Warwick. In addition, a number of colleges of advanced technology, some established as late as the 1950s, were given university status: Aston, Surrey, Bradford, Bath, Brunel, Loughborough, City University, Salford, Strathclyde and Heriot-Watt. The University College of North Staffordshire became Keele University in the 1960s and Dundee University was created from Queen's College, formerly a college of St Andrew's University. In Northern Ireland the New University of Ulster was established at Coleraine.

Some 32 polytechnics came into existence in England and Wales in the 1960s. They originated from local authority further education colleges and were established to provide degree and other advanced courses which were validated by an external body, the Council for National Academic Awards (CNAA). In 1992–93, as a result of 1992 legislation, the polytechnics were given university status, with the power to award their own degrees, and the CNAA was abolished. In addition, two colleges of higher education in Luton and Derby also achieved university status. Similarly, four

Scottish institutions—Napier, Paisley, Robert Gordon and Glasgow Caledonian (formed from Glasgow Polytechnic and Queen's College, Glasgow)—were granted university status in 1992. In 1994 Dundee Institute of Technology became a university. In the 1980s the New University of Ulster and the Ulster Polytechnic merged to become the University of Ulster, which has campuses in Belfast, Jordanstown, Londonderry and Coleraine. The remaining higher education institutions with neither university status nor their own degree-awarding powers have their degrees validated by the Open University or other universities.

The Open University, founded in 1969, is non-residential and offers degree and other courses for adult students of all ages in Britain and some other parts of Europe (see p. 47).

## Government Responsibilities

Government funds for universities are distributed by higher education funding councils in England, Scotland and Wales (see below). In Northern Ireland this function is carried out by the Department of Education; the Northern Ireland Higher Education Council advises the Department on the planning and funding of higher education in the province in order to ensure that standards of provision are comparable with those in Great Britain. Its membership reflects academic, business, research and local community interests. The Council has close links with the English Higher Education Funding Council.

The Government reimburses the amount spent by local education authorities on mandatory student grants and fees (see p. 57).

### Funding Councils

The funding councils are responsible for financing teaching and general research. Their members are appointed by the

Government and are drawn from universities, industry and commerce.

Funds for teaching are based on student numbers and are distributed under a formula designed to promote efficiency and stability. The councils also set aside sums each year to support particular proposals and initiatives. Funds to support research are allocated largely by reference to quality.

Funding councils are responsible for monitoring the financial health of universities and colleges. This includes checking and analysing:

—audited annual accounts;

—annually prepared financial forecasts covering the five-year period ahead; and

—a detailed annual breakdown of the information in the audited accounts.

Councils' Audit Services are responsible for promoting good management practice and value for money within higher education institutions and the councils themselves. They also provide advice on all audit matters within higher education.

*Quality of Education*

The funding councils have a statutory duty to assess the quality of education provided by universities and colleges. The English and Scottish Councils have committees which advise on the discharge of this duty. In England the Quality Assessment Division is responsible for carrying out assessments. Assessors appointed to work with the Division's permanent staff are recruited mainly from higher education institutions and, where relevant, industry, commerce and the professions.

The assessment process has three main elements:

—an up-to-date self-critical analysis by institutions of the education they provide;

—examination of this by the assessors; and

—independent judgement, which may involve a visit by a team of assessors.

Similar arrangements apply to the Welsh and Scottish Higher Education Funding Councils. In Scotland a team will make a visit in order to carry out an assessment.

The English Higher Education Council advises the Department of Education regarding the universities in Northern Ireland.

The funding councils are obliged to publish regular reports on the quality of education and aim to ensure that any serious problems are put right by the institution concerned. Reports are available from the councils.

In future, funding councils will arrange for the publication of information about the performance of universities and colleges, including their degree results and the number of graduates who obtain employment.

### Higher Education Quality Council

The Higher Education Quality Council (HEQC), established in May 1992 and financed by subscriptions from universities and other institutions of higher education, also helps to improve quality by checking that the institutions have satisfactory quality assurance systems. Council reports comment on areas of good practice and make suggestions for improvement for consideration by the university or college. Reports are published and a response is required from institutions. The reports are available to the public.

# University Government

Every university established prior to 1992 has a chancellor as its titular head, who may preside at meetings of the university governing body and at degree-giving ceremonies. It is an honorary, largely ceremonial, appointment.

The vice-chancellor (principal and vice-chancellor in Scotland) is the chief academic and administrative officer and is responsible for the day-to-day running of the university. The registrar or secretary is in charge of the administration.

In England and Wales the Council is the main body involved in university government. At least 50 per cent of its members come from outside the university as a result of links between the university, the local education authority and business. This group also contains distinguished people able and willing to take part in university government. The other 50 per cent of members are largely academic staff plus a limited number of people representing students and non-academic staff. The Council is responsible for staff appointments and promotions, allocating resources and bidding for finance from external sources such as the Government, research councils and industry and commerce. Similar arrangements exist in Northern Ireland.

In Scotland higher education institutions are run by a governing body commonly known as the Court, which normally consists of 20–25 members including representatives from industry, commerce, the professions and education, as well as senior officers, academic staff, students and non-academic staff. The Court chairperson is appointed from among the lay members. Students at the universities of Aberdeen, Edinburgh, Glasgow and St Andrew's elect a Rector who serves for three years as chairperson of the Court.

Each governing body appoints a Senate or Academic Council to deal with the planning, co-ordination, development and supervision of the institution's work. Chaired by the vice-chancellor, the Senate consists of academic staff and a limited number of student representatives. It is concerned with the academic activities of the institution, including admissions policy, curricula, examinations, research facilities and libraries.

In some institutions, graduates may form an organisation entitled to make nominations to the governing body and to make representations to it on any aspects of the university's affairs.

Each institution has a professional administration responsible for all non-academic activities, including financial accounting, upkeep of buildings and capital investment.

The universities of London and Wales are federal universities; each college has its own system of government similar to that of the other universities. The constituent colleges of Cambridge and Oxford Universities are independent and self-governing with their own property, income and statutes. Both universities have a general board composed of elected academics with responsibility for academic matters. At Cambridge a financial board co-ordinates finance and the Council of the Senate is responsible for administration. Responsibility for finance at Oxford University is shared by the general board and the Hebdomadal Council, which is the University's main policy and executive body.

For universities established following the 1992 Further and Higher Education Act, the Board of Governors is responsible for determining the educational character and purpose of the institution and for overseeing its activities. The Board also has to secure a balanced budget, use resources efficiently and effectively, make sure that the institution is solvent and safeguard its assets. Boards of Governors are small executive-style bodies and at least half of their members are independent members with commercial, industrial or professional experience. Academic matters are the responsibility of an Academic Board. The Principal and the Board of Governors are responsible for overall management.

## Committee of Vice-Chancellors and Principals

The executive heads of all universities form the Committee of Vice-Chancellors and Principals of the Universities of the United Kingdom, whose main functions are to:

—formulate policy on matters affecting universities;

—represent universities when dealing with the Government, Parliament and other organisations;

—provide information, advice and assistance to universities; and

—take part in national negotiations with trade unions on salaries and other conditions of service.

The Committee is financed from annual subscriptions paid by member institutions on a formula which is in part related to the size of the institution.

## Association of Commonwealth Universities

Nearly all British universities are members of the Association of Commonwealth Universities (ACU) founded in 1913. It provides an administrative link between member universities as well as certain central services. The ACU is controlled by a council of vice-chancellors, presidents or principals representing member universities in the different Commonwealth countries. It is the oldest international association of universities in the world.

The ACU's aims are to:

—promote contact and co-operation between member institutions;

—encourage and support the movement of academic/administra-
tive staff and students from one Commonwealth country to
another; and

—organise meetings of various kinds.

## Entrance Requirements

Higher education institutions normally set minimum entrance
requirements for degree courses. Many formal qualifications are
acceptable and some mature students can be admitted without such
qualifications. Many institutions take into account previous experience and non-traditional qualifications when accepting students.

In England and Wales passes at GCE A and AS level are one
of the most common requirements for entry, some courses requiring passes in specific subjects. Two or three A level grades A to C
or equivalent passes are usually required to secure a university
place.

Wider access for students to higher education courses is being
encouraged. Credit accumulation and transfer arrangements, oper-
ated by many institutions, provide students with greater flexibility
in their studies by enabling them to transfer between courses or
between institutions without repeating work or levels of study.

In Scotland access to higher education is commonly depen-
dent upon appropriate Scottish Certificate of Education examination passes, usually obtained before leaving school. Equivalent
qualifications obtained after leaving school are also considered. In
1988 the Government launched the Scottish Wider Access
Programme (SWAP) to promote access to higher education for
adults lacking traditional qualifications. Particular emphasis was
placed upon members of under-represented groups such as ethnic
minorities, women wishing to make a career in engineering and

technology, people suffering from disabilities and economically deprived people. Students successfully completing a SWAP course are guaranteed access to higher education and about 8 per cent of all entries to higher education are via access courses. In 1989–90 about 750 mature students enrolled on SWAP courses, this number rising to over 2,000 in 1993–94. Support funding for SWAP expired at the end of July 1994; a review is being undertaken by the Scottish Office Education Department.

Formal academic qualifications are not required to register for most courses at the Open University, although the standard of degrees is the same as those of other universities. The academic year begins in February and applications have to be sent in by the previous September. Places are allocated on a 'first come, first served' basis. Applications are made direct to the University and not through the independent Universities and Colleges Admissions Service (UCAS).

## Applications and Information

Applications for undergraduate places in universities are dealt with by UCAS. This gives all applicants, irrespective of gender, age, religion, ethnic origin or educational background, the opportunity to choose courses in an informed manner. The UCAS scheme has to be used for all applications for entry to full-time and sandwich undergraduate degree courses to universities and some colleges affiliated to universities. The UCAS application form offers applicants a maximum of eight choices. Each institution has the right to choose its own students and produces a prospectus outlining full details of the facilities and courses offered. UCAS publishes a handbook listing all courses, as well as *University and College Entrance*, which provides more information, including entry requirements.

The UCAS scheme is backed up by the Government's computerised information service (ECCTIS), covering over 80,000 courses in universities and colleges. There are 4,000 access points in Britain and interntionally. ECCTIS is also available on personal computers through compact disc. ECCTIS enables people to discover which institutions offer particular subjects or combinations of subjects. It works closely with UCAS, whose handbook is available on the database.

Application forms have to be completed and sent to UCAS between 1 September and 15 December for courses beginning in October of the next year. Applicants who include Oxford or Cambridge Universities in their choices must in addition apply separately to those institutions. Applicants are not permitted to change their choices after the form has been sent to UCAS.

Once the forms are received by UCAS, it forwards copies simultaneously to the institutions named on the form. In turn, they take their decisions on applications independently of each other and send them to UCAS, which provides a statement to the applicants setting out details of these decisions. These normally take the form of conditional offers requiring the applicant to obtain specified grades in forthcoming examinations.

Applicants are entitled to hold two conditional offers. If the applicant fulfils the preferred offer's conditions, he or she will be given a place in the institution concerned. The second offer is held as an insurance, normally with less demanding conditions. Consequently, if the applicant fails to meet the conditions of the preferred offer but does so with the second offer, he or she is given a place.

UCAS operates a clearing-house scheme in August–September each year to match vacancies with those applicants who are still unplaced. It allows them to re-apply where places are available, usually at a university or college other than their original choice.

There is a different system for people applying for postgraduate places. Application forms are available from the appropriate faculty office.

## Courses and Qualifications

Higher education institutions offer a wide variety of courses ranging from medicine, law, science, engineering and computing to health care, architecture, history, languages, art and design, music and drama and training for teaching and other professions. Most courses are offered on a full-time basis, but an increasing number are part-time, where study is undertaken either by attending the institution or by means of distance learning.

Many courses, especially in science and engineering, are of the sandwich type, enabling students to intersperse formal study with periods of professional training or work experience in a professional environment or in industry. These courses normally take a year longer to complete than regular full-time courses. Other vocational courses have business or industrial placements, where the student is given practical problems to tackle and has to devise and explain solutions to industrial and academic tutors.

Higher education courses in England, Wales and Northern Ireland consist of:

—first (bachelor) degrees;

—postgraduate degrees (masters and doctorates); and

—professional qualifications.

Most first degree courses take three years, with the exception of language courses and a few others where an additional year is spent abroad, or those involving industrial training which last four years. Degree courses in some professional subjects such as medicine, dentistry and veterinary medicine take five or six years' study. In Scotland most first degrees are four-year courses.

First degrees in most institutions have the title Bachelor of Arts (BA) or Bachelor of Science (BSc). Special qualifications are sometimes awarded for bachelor degrees in engineering (BEng) and education (BEd). Where degrees are awarded with honours, these are divided into four classes: first, upper second, lower second and third.

A typical academic year begins in the autumn and is usually divided into three terms, but more flexible patterns of teaching and learning are being introduced and there is considerable variety between institutions. Some have chosen a two-term year while others are experimenting with more intensive two-year first degrees.

Masters degrees, requiring one or two years' study, are titled according to the area of study: Master of Arts (MA), Master of Science (MSc) or Master of Philosophy (MPhil).

The degree of Doctor of Philosophy is awarded for original research over a period of three years or more in all subjects.

In Scotland the traditional first degree in the arts, humanities and languages has been the Master of Arts (MA). For the sciences, engineering, divinity and many of the social sciences, the traditional first degree is a Bachelor's degree. The latter title has been adopted for the majority of first degrees developed over the last 30 years irrespective of academic discipline.

Universities and a number of other higher education institutions offer their own degrees, while other institutions have their degrees validated by a university or other degree-awarding higher education institutions. The Open University has a national validation service.

Degree courses are increasingly organised on a course unit system, involving studying and passing a set number of units or half units over a given time. This allows students to combine, for instance, a foreign language with subjects like law and business studies. Linked with this are credit and accumulation schemes giving freedom to move from one institution to another in Britain and elsewhere in Europe to achieve the number of modules required for the degree.

## Open University

The Open University, Britain's largest university, provides opportunities to many who would not otherwise participate in higher education. There are no formal entry requirements for most courses. Three-quarters of students have jobs and study on a part-time basis. In 1994 there were some 91,000 registered undergraduates, and in all some 155,000 first degrees have been awarded since the University opened in 1970.

The University is best known for its undergraduate programme. Its first degree is the BA (Open) and the BSc (Open) which are general degrees awarded on a system of credits for each course completed. Courses are either 60 points or 30 points on a scale. A total of 360 points is required for the award of a first degree. Although it is possible to graduate in three years, most students take between four and six years. The University has reached agreements with many other universities under which holders of Open credits can transfer to full-time courses elsewhere and vice versa.

Most Open University undergraduates begin with a foundation course providing a general introduction to teaching methods and covering one of five academic areas: arts, mathematics and computing, science, social sciences and technology. Beyond foundation level, undergraduate courses involve study at three levels of progressively higher academic standards.

Much of the studying on all courses takes place at home, students using specially written texts, television and radio, and video/audio cassettes. The radio and television programmes are broadcast on the BBC national networks. Home experiment kits are used for courses calling for practical work, while computers are used increasingly in a wide range of courses.

The 13 Open University regional centres—in London, East Grinstead, Oxford, Bristol, Birmingham, Nottingham, Cambridge, Leeds, Manchester, Newcastle, Cardiff, Edinburgh and Belfast—manage some 270 local study centres which provide tutorial and counselling support. All registered students have a local tutor and counsellor who is based at one of the study centres. The regions employ some 7,000 teaching and counselling staff. In addition, there are one-week residential schools held in the summer months and shorter weekend schools throughout the year.

Students do not qualify for mandatory grants from local education authorities (see p. 57). Some authorities assist with residential school fees and employers will often provide help, especially if the courses are relevant to the student's job or occupation. The University, too, has financial award schemes for unemployed students or for those on low incomes. Fees can be paid by instalments.

The University has a programme of higher degrees, including the Master of Business Administration and an MA in education.

There are also programmes for professionals in education, health and welfare services; other courses are for managers, scientists and technologists. Some of these are presented as multi-media courses while others are in the form of self-contained study packs. The University regards research work as a vital part of its activities and offers research-based degree courses.

A recent development is a part-time initial teacher training programme which combines distance teaching methods with secondments to local schools for practical experience. The first 1,300 students enrolled on this course in 1994.

The University has advised many other countries on setting up similar institutions. It operates throughout Western Europe, admitting students of all nationalities to study its English courses. In Eastern Europe and the Commonwealth of Independent States the University is working in partnership with local institutions who translate the courses into the indigenous language and supervise the teaching. Managers in Russia, Hungary, the Czech Republic, Slovakia, Bulgaria and Romania are currently studying with the Open Business School.

There are more than 6,000 non-United Kingdom students registered on Open University courses.

## Teacher Training

Some higher education institutions specialise in initial teacher training courses. In order to obtain Qualified Teacher Status, there are two main degree routes:

—the four-year Bachelor of Education (BEd) degree; or

—a three-year relevant subject degree, followed by a one-year Postgraduate Certificate in Education (PGCE), in which most of the time is spent training in schools.

In September 1993 a number of school consortia began providing their own courses of initial teacher training for postgraduates. These courses lead to Qualified Teacher Status.

Under the provisions of the 1994 Education Act in England and Wales, schools will play a much larger part in initial teacher training by taking on more responsibility for planning and managing courses and for the selection, training and assessment of students, usually in partnership with institutions. They will train students to teach their specialist subjects, assess pupils and manage classes; they will also supervise students and assess their competence.

Consortia of schools will be able to run courses for postgraduate students if they wish to do so. Other courses, including all undergraduate courses, will be run by universities and colleges in partnership with schools.

From 1995–96, the Teacher Training Agency, established by the 1994 Education Act, will finance initial teacher training courses, ensure that national standards are met and promote teaching as a career. The Agency's objectives include:

—helping to raise teaching standards;

—improving the quality and efficiency of all routes into the teaching profession; and

—securing the involvement of schools in all training courses.

In Wales, responsibility for funding initial teacher training will remain with the Higher Education Funding Council for Wales, which will also be able to fund such training in schools.

Teacher training in Scotland is provided in specialist teacher education institutions and certain university faculties of education. Initial teacher training courses are approved by the Secretary of State and must conform to national guidelines. All courses are subject to professional accreditation by the General Teaching Council for Scotland. Funding for teacher training is provided via the Scottish Higher Education Funding Council.

In Northern Ireland, teacher training is provided by Stranmillis College, St Mary's College, Queen's University Belfast and the University of Ulster. The main courses are the four-year BEd Honours, BA Honours (Education) and the one-year Postgraduate Certificate of Education. Teacher training arrangements are currently under review but will take account of the broad thrust of national policy developments. The education and library boards have a duty to ensure that teachers are equipped with the necessary skills to implement education reforms and the Northern Ireland Curriculum.

### Other Professions

A degree or diploma is essential for many careers and occupations such as architecture, law, medicine, chartered engineering, librarianship and teaching.

## Academic Research

Universities are among the main centres for academic research in science, technology, social sciences, the arts and other subjects.

Government responsibilities for science and technology are carried out by the Office of Science and Technology (OST) within the Cabinet Office. The OST is headed by the Government's Chief Scientific Adviser. A Cabinet minister is responsible for science policy.

The OST funds research by:

—grants and contracts to universities and other higher education establishments through the research councils (see below); and

—support for postgraduate study.

The OST administers the LINK scheme, which encourages co-operation between research councils and industry. It is responsible for a number of Government-funded research councils, which in 1994 are being reorganised into six councils in order to respond to the rapid pace of change in science and technology. Each council is autonomous, with members of its governing body drawn from the universities, the professions, industry and Government. The six councils are as follows:

1. *The Engineering and Physical Sciences Research Council*, which supports research and postgraduate training in chemistry, mathematics, physics, information and manufacturing technology and engineering.

2. *The Particle Physics and Astronomy Research Council*, which is concerned with particle physics, astronomy and study of the solar system.

3. *The Biotechnology and Biological Sciences Research Council*, which supports research underpinning industries like agriculture, food, biotechnology, pharmaceuticals, chemicals and health care.

4. *The Medical Research Council*, which is the Government's main agency supporting medical research.

5. *The Natural Environment Research Council*, which undertakes and helps finance research in marine, earth, terrestrial, freshwater, polar and atmospheric sciences.

6. *The Economic and Social Research Council*, which supports social science research in areas like economics, education, environment and planning, management, politics, psychology and sociology.

**University Contribution**

About 40 per cent of research carried out in universities in England, Wales and Scotland is financed by the higher education funding councils. These funds contribute to the cost of academic staff and pay for support staff, administration, equipment and accommodation. They focus mainly on basic and strategic research.

The other main channels are the research councils, government departments, charities and industry, which fund particular projects. Substantial funding also comes from European Union programmes. Universities are expected to recover the full cost of short-term commissioned research from the Government and industry.

The high quality of research in universities, and their marketing skills, have enabled them to attract more funding from a wider range of external sources, the main growth in income arising from contracts with industry.

There are around 40 science parks at or near universities. These are partnerships between higher education institutions and industry to promote commercially focused research, often involving advanced technology. The parks provide accommodation for over 1,000 companies. Most are engaged in computing, electronics, instrumentation, robotics, electrical engineering, chemicals and biotechnology. The largest science park is at Cambridge, where there are 85 companies on site.

A growing number of universities offer industry interdisciplinary research centres, including access to analytical equipment, library facilities and worldwide databases as well as academic expertise.

## Students

Students can expect to have access to full information about their courses and how they are taught and assessed. Universities and colleges should explain the structure of the course, its aims, the qualification received and opportunities to proceed to further study. Under the Charters for Higher Education, opportunities should be offered to student representatives to take part in decision-taking on academic matters.

In the first few days of the academic year, the university or college provides information about the services available on site. These include:

—proper counselling for illness and stress;

—medical help;

—arrangements for student security;

—careers advice; and

—recreation, including sport.

**Life as a Student**

All institutions have an accommodation unit to help students find somewhere to live. This may range from the institution's own accommodation (halls of residence and self-catering flats) to private houses and flats, lodgings and hostels.

Specialist counselling services give advice to students on problems regarding choice of course and other academic matters. Counsellors also deal with personal problems, such as worries over academic work and examinations.

Many institutions have a chaplaincy centre used by different Christian groups for meetings, services and prayer. The chaplains work as an ecumenical team. Rabbis often act as Chaplain for Jewish students. Other non-Christian religions are catered for, some universities having Muslim cultural and religious centres.

Every institution has free medical and nursing services, ranging from first aid to cancer screening and general advice on health and diet.

A wide variety of services support teaching, learning and research. These include library, information, audio-visual media and reprographic services. Well stocked libraries not only hold books and academic journals but also provide access to computer-based information and specialised collections.

Central computer systems are usually available 24 hours a day, seven days a week, throughout the campus. Britain's Joint Academic Network (JANET) currently links 200 sites and has served universities and research institutes for more than a decade. The higher education funding councils and the Department of Education for Northern Ireland are funding the SuperJANET network, designed to transmit information faster than any previously available; it can, for example, transmit the equivalent of a 5,500-page report in less than one second. A pilot SuperJANET network has been established connecting sites in Cambridge, Edinburgh, Manchester, London, Oxford and the two universities in Northern Ireland. Initially, the new network will include high-performance computing, distance learning, electronic publishing, library document distribution, multi-media information services and visual–voice contacts between researchers. Many of these systems are linked to databases in other countries.

Another important service helps students find jobs once they graduate. University career teams organise seminars and workshops on topics such as interview techniques. Some organise annual careers information fairs and encourage employers' recruitment programmes on campus.

Students organise clubs and societies covering all kinds of subjects and interests, including sport, drama, debating, music, religion and politics. Many have their own choirs and orchestras. Some universities have arts centres and theatres open to the local public.

Many institutions have their own sports fields, catering for many sports such as athletics, hockey, football, rugby and cricket. Other facilities include gymnasia, swimming pools and tennis courts.

### Student Unions

Every university has a students' union or association which organises recreational facilities and entertainments, provides a range of bars and food outlets and offers welfare, financial and travel services. The union also represents student interests in discussions with the university administration and is represented on governing committees.

Under the 1994 Education Act, university or college governing bodies will have to ensure that the student union operates in a fair and democratic manner. In addition the union will be required to have a written constitution approved by the governing body and subject to review by that body every five years. Students will have the right not to be a member of the union. Appointment to major union offices will be made by secret ballot of union members and the governing body will ensure that these elections are fairly and properly conducted. The governing body will also monitor union expenditure. Financial reports of the union will be published annually and made available to the governing body and to all students. Any affiliation by a union to external bodies will be decided by a secret ballot of union members and be subject to annual review.

The National Union of Students acts as a pressure group on behalf of student interests. Its members are drawn from the affiliated student unions in universities and colleges.

### Complaints Systems

Under the Government's Charter for Higher Education, students are entitled to complain about services provided for them by universities and other higher education establishments. They have an internal complaints system and many allow students to raise academic matters of concern to them. If disputes cannot be sorted out internally, or if students feel that that they have not received a fair hearing, many institutions bring in someone from outside to deal with disputes.

A complaint may be made to the Higher Education Quality Council if it concerns misleading information in a prospectus and the student is not satisfied with the outcome of the internal complaints system.

The 1994 Education Act makes provision for a complaints procedure for individuals or groups of students dissatisfied in their dealings with the student union; this will include provision for the governing body to appoint an independent person to investigate and report on complaints. Effective remedies will be available if a complaint is upheld.

### Student Grants and Loans

Students resident in Britain who are on a full-time higher education course, including a sandwich course, can get financial support in the form of awards and loans. This also applies to students on a part-time course of initial teacher training. Another source of help is the access fund maintained by each university or college (see below).

Awards are paid by local education authorities in England and Wales. They consist of a means-tested grant which helps pay living costs and a payment which meets the costs of tuition. Parents are expected to contribute towards the grant if their income is above a certain level. LEAs require students to complete a grant application form and a grant assessment form so that the local education authority can decide how much the student should receive for living costs. Students who receive an unconditional offer of a college place must also complete the college acceptance form and return it to the institution. The college completes the form and returns it to the local education authority. Fees or grant are not paid by the local education authority until it receives this form.

The Government finances non-means-tested loans to students. The scheme is administered by the Student Loans Company. Application forms are available from the university or college, which has to certify that the student is eligible for a loan. Applications are made once during each academic year and loan agreements have to be signed and returned to the Company by 31 July. The loan is paid back to the Company in monthly instalments after completion of the course; interest on the loan is linked with inflation, the amount owed being adjusted each year in line with the Retail Prices Index. Repayments can be deferred for a year at a time if the person's income is not more than 85 per cent of national average earnings. An independent assessor is responsible for investigating disagreements between the student and the Company.

Each university or college has a limited access fund which provides selective help at its discretion to full-time students with serious financial difficulties or to those unable to afford higher education. The institution decides which students should receive payments and how much each payment should be. It also handles any appeals against a refusal to help. Students must be able to show that they need help and they have explored other ways of supporting themselves. If eligible for a student loan, this must normally be taken out before any application is made to an access fund.

In Northern Ireland, access funds for students attending further education colleges are held by the education and library boards rather than the colleges.

## Sponsorship

Some students are given financial support by employers and other organisations. This enables employers to begin training their staff at an earlier stage. In a few cases the student is paid an annual salary but in most cases he or she works for the employer for about three or four months in the year and receives a grant from the local education authority with a supplement from the employer. It is also possible to spend a year in industry before entering university or college, either with or without sponsorship. Sponsorship is usually provided for courses in engineering, specialised science subjects, business studies and related subjects.

There is also a system of Career Development Loans which support one-year courses in a wide range of vocational areas, provided that the student does not have financial help from an employer or a full mandatory award. Managed by the Employment Department, these schemes are run through a partnership with a number of high street banks. The loan covers course fees, costs such as books and materials, and, if the course is full-time, living expenses.

## Study in Europe

The European Union has a number of programmes designed to ease the movement of students between member states and to help meet their education and training needs.

The largest of these is the ERASMUS programme, which enables students to study anywhere in the European Union or in Austria, Finland, Iceland, Liechtenstein, Norway, Sweden or Switzerland for a period of 3 to 12 months. Grants are provided to universities and other higher educational institutions to develop student mobility programmes and top-up grants are paid to students to help cover the extra costs of study in another country, including return fares and differences in the cost of living.

The LINGUA Programme aims to improve the teaching and learning of foreign languages in education, training and working life. Grants are payable to help meet the cost of studying elsewhere in the European Union for between three months and a year.

Another important programme is COMETT, which develops co-operation between higher education institutions and industrial enterprises on training. Placements for between 3 and 12 months are funded through COMETT and are arranged by partnerships of local higher education institutions and industrial firms. Companies pay the salaries of their participating employees and COMETT meets the costs of travel expenses and attending a language course.

## Overseas Students

British higher education institutions and the qualifications they award have for many years attracted students from around the world. In turn overseas students have enriched academic, cultural and social life.

The number of full-time and sandwich overseas students in Great Britain attending publicly financed universities and other post-16 institutions was 99,700 in 1992–93 compared with nearly 56,600 in 1982–83. About a third of full-time overseas students come from other European Union member states.

Overseas students wishing to follow a first degree or under-graduate course require a good command of written and spoken English and usually have to pass a language test. Many universities and colleges offer English courses between July and September to help students whose English needs to be improved before starting their studies. In addition, many British institutions conduct special pre-degree courses designed to bridge the gap between overseas qualifications and the usual requirements for entry to British degree courses.

Applications for first degree courses are usually made through UCAS (see p. 43) and forms have to be completed and received by 15 December in the year before courses begin.

Engineering and technology, social science and business/financial studies are the most popular subject groups for overseas students.

Several London University degrees, mainly in the arts and social sciences, may be taken by external students throughout the world. Although there is no formal tuition, the University provides learning materials, short courses on particular topics and informal tutorial assessment. Students are able to register and sit examinations in most countries. The minimum period of study is three years, although in practice students tend to take longer. Further information is available from the Secretary for External Students, University of London.

The British Government makes considerable provision for foreign students and trainees in its aid programme and through other award and scholarship schemes. In 1992–93 some 21,000 were supported at a cost of £147 million.

The Foreign and Commonwealth Office finances the British Chevening Scholarships, a worldwide programme offering outstanding graduate students and young professionals the opportunity to spend a formative part of their careers studying at British universities and other academic institutions. In 1994–95 some £30 million is being spent on about 5,000 scholarships for students from 146 countries.

Many public and private scholarships and fellowships are available to students from overseas and to British students who want to study overseas. Among the best known are the British Council Fellowships, the Commonwealth Scholarship and Fellowship Plan, the Fulbright Scholarship Scheme, the Marshall Scholarships, the Rhodes Scholarships and the Churchill Scholarships.

The increasing interest in English as a foreign language is reflected in the growth of English language courses in publicly funded institutions and in the number of private language schools in Britain. Over 240 private schools and over 60 state colleges are accredited by the British Council for the teaching of English as a foreign language.

The British Council, which is independent and non-political, promotes educational, cultural and technical co-operation between Britain and other countries. It is represented in nearly 100 countries, where its offices provide information and advice on all aspects of British education.

The United Kingdom Council for Overseas Student Affairs (UKCOSA) is a registered charity concerned with the welfare and interests of overseas students in Britain. Students can usually contact UKCOSA through the welfare officer or adviser at their university or students' union.

Each institution has some form of medical and nursing service. If studying in Britain for more than six months, overseas students are entitled to medical care under Britain's National Health Service.

# Addresses

Adult Literacy and Basic Skills Unit, Kingsbourne House, 229/31 High Holborn, London WC1V 7DA.

Association of Commonwealth Universities, 36 Gordon Square, London WC1H 0PF.

Business & Technology Education Council, Central House, Upper Woburn Place, London WC1H 0HH.

British Council, 10 Spring Gardens, London SW1A 2BN.

City and Guilds of London Institute, 76 Portland Place, London WC1N 4AA.

Committee of Vice-Chancellors and Principals of the United Kingdom Universities, 29 Tavistock Square, London WC1H 9EZ.

Department for Education, Sanctuary Buildings, Great Smith Street, London SW1P 3BT.

Department of Education for Northern Ireland, Rathgael House, Balloo Road, Bangor, County Down BT12 2PR.

Further Education Funding Council for England, Cheylesmore House, Quinton Road, Coventry CV1 2WT.

Further Education Funding Council for Wales, Lambourne House, Cardiff Business Park, Llanishen, Cardiff CF4 5GL.

Higher Education Funding Council for England, Northavon House, Coldharbour Lane, Bristol, BS18 1QD.

Higher Education Funding Council for Scotland, Donaldson House, 97 Haymarket Terrace, Edinburgh EH12 5HD.

Higher Education Funding Council for Wales, Labourne House, Cardiff Business Park, Llanishen, Cardiff CF4 5GL.

National Council for Vocational Qualifications, 222 Euston Road, London NW1 2BZ.

National Organisation for Adult Learning, 21 De Montfort Street, Leicester LE1 7GE.

Office of Public Service and Science, Cabinet Office, 70 Whitehall, London SW1A 2AS.

RSA Examinations Board, Westwood Way, Coventry CV4 8HS.

Scottish Examinations Board, Ironmills House, Dalkeith EH22 1LE.

Scottish Further Education Unit, Jordanhill Campus, University of Strathclyde, Southbrae Drive, Glasgow G13 1PP.

Scottish Office Education Department, New St Andrew's House, Edinburgh EH1 3TG.

Scottish Vocational Education Council, Hanover House, 24 Douglas Street, Glasgow G2 7NQ.

School Curriculum and Assessment Authority, Newcombe House, 45 Notting Hill Gate, London W11 3JB.

Students Loans Company, Limited, 100 Bothwell Street, Glasgow G2 7JD.

Universities and Colleges Admissions Service, Fulton House, Jessup Avenue, Cheltenham GL50 3SH.

United Kingdom Council for Overseas Student Affairs, 17/19 St Albans Place, London N1 0NX.

Welsh Office, Cathays Park, Cardiff CF1 3NQ.

Workers' Educational Association, Temple House, 17 Victoria Park Square, London E2 9PB.

# Index

Printed in the United Kingdom for HMSO.
Dd.0298449, 2/95, C30, 56–6734, 5673